Authentic Assessment

The Practicing Administrator's Leadership Series
Jerry J. Herman and Janice L. Herman, Editors

ROADMAPS
TO SUCCESS

Other Titles in This Series Include:

The Path to School Leadership: A Portable Mentor
Lee G. Bolman and Terrence E. Deal

Holistic Quality: Managing, Restructuring, and Empowering Schools
Jerry J. Herman

Selecting, Managing, and Marketing Technologies
Jamieson A. McKenzie

Individuals With Disabilities: Implementing the Newest Laws
Patricia F. First and Joan L. Curcio

Violence in the Schools: How to Proactively Prevent and Defuse It
Joan L. Curcio and Patricia F. First

Women in Administration: Facilitators for Change
L. Nan Restine

Power Learning in the Classroom
Jamieson A. McKenzie

Computers: Literacy and Learning
A Primer for Administrators
George E. Marsh II

Restructuring Schools: Doing It Right
Mike M. Milstein

Reporting Child Abuse:
A Guide to Mandatory Requirements for School Personnel
Karen L. Michaelis

Handbook on Gangs in Schools:
Strategies to Reduce Gang-Related Activities
Shirley R. Lal, Dhyan Lal, and Charles M. Achilles

Conflict Resolution: Building Bridges
Neil H. Katz and John W. Lawyer

Resolving Conflict Successfully: Needed Knowledge and Skills
Neil H. Katz and John W. Lawyer

Preventing and Managing Conflict in Schools
Neil H. Katz and John W. Lawyer

Secrets of Highly Effective Meetings
Maria M. Shelton and Laurie K. Bauer

(see back cover for additional titles)

Authentic Assessment

A Guide to Implementation

Cheryl Fulton Fischer
Rita M. King

CORWIN PRESS, INC.
A Sage Publications Company
Thousand Oaks, California

LB
3051
.F55
1995

For information address:

Corwin Press, Inc.
A Sage Publications Company
2455 Teller Road
Thousand Oaks, California 91320

SAGE Publications Ltd.
6 Bonhill Street
London EC2A 4PU
United Kingdom

SAGE Publications India Pvt. Ltd.
M-32 Market
Greater Kailash I
New Delhi 110 048 India

Printed in the United States of America

Library of Congress Cataloging-in-Publication Data

Fischer, Cheryl Fulton.
    Authentic assessment : a guide to implementation / Cheryl Fulton Fischer, Rita M. King.
        p.   cm. — (Roadmaps to success)
    Includes bibliographical references.
    ISBN 0-8039-6256-8 (pbk.)
        1. Educational tests and measurements—United States.   I. King, Rita M.   II. Title.   III. Series.
    LB3051.F55   1995
    371.2'6'0973—dc20   95-1898

This book is printed on acid-free paper.

95 96 97 98 99 10 9 8 7 6 5 4 3 2 1

Corwin Press Production Editor: S. Marlene Head

Contents

Management System for the Portfolio System
• Integrating Authentic Assessment Into
Instruction • Integrating Problem-Solving and
Communication Skills • The Teacher's Role in
Guiding the Learning • Evaluating Student Work
• The Issue of Grading • How to Start

Foreword

A*uthentic assessment* is a key concept that is finding its way into numerous school districts and thousands of classrooms. It is being implemented in response to the belief that national norm-referenced tests are invalid and/or incomplete measures by which to judge the achievement level of many students—especially minority students.

Cheryl Fischer and Rita King have authored a brief, easily read book, titled *Authentic Assessment: A Guide to Implementation*, to assist in understanding the methods of implementing this concept. Within the book's chapters, they discuss the problems associated with traditional student testing practices, and they stress the advantages of moving to authentic assessment techniques.

Furthermore, they elaborate on the teacher's role in authentic assessment approaches, and they divulge the means for developing and implementing an authentic assessment program at the school district, school building, or individual classroom level. They also discuss the administrator's role in developing and maintaining an authentic assessment program. Finally, they offer a series of helpful hints on how to involve students, parents, and community members in the learning process.

Whether, as a teacher or an administrator, you are contemplating going into an authentic assessment approach to student assessment, are already involved in an authentic assessment program that could be improved, or simply want to understand more about the topic, this guidebook will prove invaluable. The authors have also included an annotated bibliography of helpful sources of information if you wish to delve more deeply into this subject.

JERRY J. HERMAN
JANICE L. HERMAN
Series Co-Editors

About the Authors

Cheryl Fulton Fischer is an Associate Professor in the Educational Administration Program in the School of Education at California State University San Bernardino. She has been involved in education since 1968 in a variety of teaching and administrative roles, including those of classroom teacher in diverse settings at the elementary, middle, and high school levels; district curriculum specialist; school site administrator; adjunct professor; and assistant superintendent for instruction. She has trained teachers at the college level, and currently trains future school administrators and teaches graduate-level courses in administration, curriculum, and supervision of instruction. She received her B.Ed. and M.Ed. from the University of Hawaii and her Ph.D. from Claremont Graduate School in California. Dr. Fischer has also served as a consultant and advisor to school districts, county offices, and the state department of education, as well as to school boards and industry. She has presented her work extensively at local, state, and national conferences and for professional organizations. Her broad experience as a practitioner, coupled with her research work, enables her to prepare materials that are useful for today's educators. In addition to her interest and expertise in the development and implementation of performance assessment and alternative forms of instruction, she has distinguished herself through her work in designing effective educational programs for at-risk and homeless students.

Rita M. King is an Assistant Professor working with Educational Administration in the Gladys L. Benerd School of Education at the University of the Pacific, Stockton, CA. She has been a classroom teacher, principal of a year-round elementary school, and district director of curriculum, and she was a coordinator in curriculum, instruction, and staff development for county school offices in Ohio and California. She has also worked as a visiting educator with the California Department of Education and was researcher, reviewer, and editor of a catalog of critical and creative thinking materials. Dr. King has authored two books and numerous other works. She has extensive experience in planning, organizing, and leading staff development—including facilitating school leadership teams and staff retreats; helping school systems understand brain-based learning and cognitive coaching; and helping educators build their decision-making capacity through action research, total quality, and continual improvement efforts. Dr. King is the 1994-1995 president of the California Association of Professors of Educational Administration (CAPEA). She is a member of the California Collaborative for Educational Leadership, which is a partnership of several statewide organizations designed to integrate leadership preparation and development efforts in California, and serves on the boards of the California Staff Development Council (CSDC) and the State of California Association for Teacher Education (SCATE). Her doctoral degree was earned at the University of San Diego.

Traditional Testing Practices Versus Authentic Assessment

In a survey on "The Changing Face of Testing and Assessment," more than half of the respondents (53%) claimed to have made significant changes in their testing programs during the preceding 5 years (Hymes, 1991). Testing is being scrutinized closely during this decade to determine how to move beyond traditional forms of testing and to examine authentic assessment and portfolios for greater student learning, understanding, and application of knowledge.

The concept of examining students is nothing new. But what do tests achieve and for what purpose? Are traditional testing procedures appropriate for what needs to be assessed? Has knowledge increased so rapidly with the advent and continued growth of technology that it has created an urgent need for testing reform?

There are as many responses to the questions as there are people with opinions. Thus school administrators are faced more and more with questions from faculty members, parents, the community, and from students about what tests mean and about their appropriateness in specific contexts.

Therefore, this guidebook provides information for those who need information quickly and who want to understand the concept of authentic assessment. It has been created to present pertinent information in an easy-to-read format, and it is intended to be a reference for further resources.

Testing Versus Assessment

What is the difference between the terms *testing* and *assessment*? Until recently, "testing" referred to any form of measurement that yielded clear, consistent, meaningful data about a person's knowledge, aptitudes, intelligence, or other mental traits. Standardized and norm-referenced testing traditionally focuses on whether students get the "right" answers. It is not considered important to understand the process of how they arrive at their responses.

It only has been in the past few years that the term "assessment" was used in the context of appraising students. Presently, the word is used interchangeably by some with the word "testing." In the next few years, however, it is likely that the terms will become more clearly differentiated. "Assessment" more often is used with authentic, performance-based, alternative assessment systems, including portfolio assessment. Students do something other than the traditional norm-referenced or criterion-referenced paper-and-pencil measurement, requiring students not only to respond but also to demonstrate knowledge and skills.

What a student does and how the task is accomplished are major aspects of authentic assessment. Students are active participants in the learning process and become responsible for creating or constructing their responses.

Helpful Terms

There are many terms that could be defined; however, the following ones have been selected to guide the reader with a few of the terms and techniques that are used frequently when speaking of testing and assessment.

Alternative form of assessment—Assessment techniques other than the traditional norm-referenced, criterion-referenced paper-and-pencil type of tests.

Authentic assessment—An inclusive term for alternative assessment methods that examine students' ability to solve problems or perform tasks that closely resemble authentic situations.

Criterion-referenced test—A test that specifies minimum levels or standards of student performance by including questions based on what the students were taught or ought to know, thus measuring personal performance against classroom, district, or statewide criteria. Multiple choice, essay questions, or a combination of both can be used.

Demonstration—Demonstrations are often simulations of reality or demonstrations of reality itself. Students show their mastery of subject-area content and procedures by doing an active procedure that uses their newly learned skills.

Essay—A writing sample used to assess student understanding through a written description, analysis, explanation, or summary. It allows students to use facts in context and to structure a congruous presentation of those facts, demonstrating comprehension, critical thinking, analysis, and synthesis. It also can assess the skills of composition such as grammar, spelling, and syntax, as well as the structural skills of sentence and paragraph writing.

Experiment—This term often refers to how well students can carry out scientific procedures. Students actively develop hypotheses, plan and carry out experiments, write up findings, use skills of measurement and estimation, and apply scientific facts and concepts. The entire process is important to the outcome of the experiment.

Group project—A complex problem or task that requires students to work together cooperatively on planning, research, group discussion, and the ultimate presentation, performance, or product. Both the process and the outcome of the task are important in the analysis of a group project.

Norm-referenced test—An assessment instrument that measures differences among the individuals being tested. It relates the scores of each student to the scores of those in the norm group, which usually is a national norm. A norm-referenced test tells how each student and group of students measure up against the original group by distributing the range of scores along a continuum. Items tested are selected to establish whether students are above or below that norm and by what percentage.

Performance-based assessment—This type of assessment requires students to perform the actual behavior of a task rather than simply answer questions out of context. It may call for doing a piece of writing or solving mathematically or scientifically complex problems, or completing a science experiment. The performed task is then judged against established criteria.

Portfolio—A multifaceted assignment that expects more than one type of activity and production for completion and that extends over a period of time. Frequently, it requires a thematic approach to a concept. It can be a teaching tool and a form of authentic assessment. The product is reviewed according to established criteria, sometimes known as a rubric, to determine the level of student performance and progress.

Project—A comprehensive demonstration of skills or knowledge that requires a broad range of complex competencies. Frequently, projects are interdisciplinary, thematic endeavors that encourage student knowledge, creativity, initiative, and analysis.

Rubric—A standard used to determine the level of performance and progress of a student's work. Often, there are between four and six levels described, with descriptors stated for each level.

Standard—A basis or foundation established to differentiate levels of performance on a student's or group of students' test, project, activity, piece of writing, and so on.

Standardized test—A formal assessment instrument given to a large number of persons under similar conditions, designed to yield comparable scores. The term is most often applied to national norm-referenced tests developed by test publishers.

Teacher-made test—A testing or assessment procedure created by the teacher for use in the classroom. It can be norm referenced, criterion referenced, or performance based.

Why Change the Way We Test?

Standardized testing is not likely to leave the scene of American education, at least not very soon. Many people believe in its value. Most universities and colleges continue to require some form of standardized testing as a prerequisite for admission. However, there are many concerns about using only one form of testing for learning, whatever the grade level or ability of the students.

Concerns Over the Standardized Testing Approach

Over the past few years, a number of critics have leveled harsh words against standardized testing. Some of their concerns are briefly mentioned here in order to understand more clearly the reasoning behind why some seriously concerned persons have devoted great amounts of effort to developing new assessment formats:

1. *Schools and districts are not accurately reporting data.* Some test reporters have been known to be deceptive in the type of information they provide about how well a school is achieving or how successfully a student is learning.

2. *Tests do not provide clear insight into student application of knowledge.* The tests often examine meaningless and shallow facts in that they are not analyzing whether a student is capable of using the information in complex and creative thinking endeavors.

3. *Teachers often are pressured to spend excessive amounts of time on gearing up students to take tests.* Because of the increased pressures they face, teachers often work at detached, trivial tasks, such as having students drill and memorize unrelated facts; and teachers spend excessive time on those areas that they know will be tested instead of teaching a deeper and richer curriculum.

4. *Schools have felt intensive pressure to outscore and be better than other schools in their local geographical area.* Communities have been divided and pressured by the results of standardized testing that have been reported in local newspapers and by local realtors. The reported results become more consequential than the knowledge gained from the test.

5. *Students and teachers alike are politically pressured.* The testing practices in some cases have become fraudulent because of various forms of cheating that go on due to pressures placed on students and teachers to succeed.
6. *Test-construction bias exists.* There have been attacks that the tests are skewed and that many standardized tests are biased against various ethnic groups, females, limited-English-proficient students, and students who come from low-income families.
7. *Testing is very costly.* Precious district financial resources go into the testing process instead of the teaching process, taking away money that could be used to invest in classroom or school personnel or materials.

Standardized testing is useful when used appropriately. Clearly, however, other forms of assessment are necessary in an era when knowing how to make sense of information is at least as important as being able to recall facts.

The Need for a Much Greater Emphasis on Thinking

Over the past generation, the changes in governments, politics, and economics across the world have been dramatic. At the same time that knowledge continues to expand at an exponential level, new human and environmental problems continue to emerge. The signals are clear. The field of education must grow in its capacity to serve the needs of human beings as they enter a future of fast-paced change, ambiguity, the information superhighway, and potential transformation. The skills of knowing how to think through problems, how to work with constantly changing data, understanding what is necessary in making ethical decisions, recognizing how to work together on projects and needs that are larger than any one person can do, tolerating ambiguity, and patiently persisting in the face of pressure—these are just a few of the new competencies that teachers need to help students begin to achieve.

Schools cannot continue to measure for deficiencies. It is essential to meet the highest needs of all students, and that means figuring out how to help them learn to the fullest of their capacities. Administrators and teachers must communicate as professionals, design classroom learning as facilitators, and use assessment as stewards of young people's opportunities to learn. If we do less than that, we not only face the unethical abyss of failing students, but we also fail society. Every person deserves the chance to contribute and become a responsible citizen. The one consistent place that serves the citizenry of the future is the school.

It follows that if classrooms foster learning that leads to altering the outcomes that were heretofore encouraged, then the blueprint of schooling also would look very different. Table 1.1 suggests examples of how schools and classrooms can differ based on the system by which they function.

Confusion and Pressures in Testing and Assessment Communities

Just because schools and districts want to help students learn does not mean that learning happens. If it did, surely all students would be leaping forward in their progress. And just because schools and districts want to help students learn does not mean that changing to a more formative approach to assessment happens easily.

In 1989, the Governors' Commission on School Performance made several recommendations based on alternative methods of testing, saying, among other things, that those approaches measured fundamental and important areas in the curriculum; measured more than narrow, low-level objectives; encouraged material coverage beyond rote-level memorization for the test; and held schools as well as students accountable for student achievement. However, the next steps have been complex. Some states have moved forward with authentic assessment initiatives. The path has been slow, and as in the state of California in late 1994, the statewide initiative for more open-ended authentic assessment has run into roadblocks and the need for reconfiguration.

TABLE 1.1 Agendas of Schools and Classrooms Create Differences in Classroom Teaching and Instructional Practices and Supervisory Practices

Teaching and Instructional Practices	
Traditional Model	*Collaborative Model*
Teacher-centered instruction	Teacher- and student-centered instruction
Mainly teacher-driven decisions	Broader decision-making base
Lock-step scheduling	Flexible, more open scheduling
Secretive testing structures	Open, ongoing progress structures
Content separation	Thematic, integrated content
Teacher isolation	Teacher adaptation and teaming
Instructional strategies not emphasized	Emphasis on need for use of a wide variety of instructional strategies

Supervisory Practices	
Traditional Model	*Collaborative Model*
Supervisor initiated and designed	Teacher orchestrated
Data does not go solely to the teacher	Teacher maintains all data collected
Purpose is quality control	Purposes are to improve curriculum, instruction, and student learning
Deadline and resource driven	Ongoing from the first to the last day
There is a line-staff differentiation	There is no differentiation necessary in position or responsibility

It is often easier to explain what authentic assessment practices do not mean than to explain what they intend. This is a movement away from standardized tests and criterion-referenced tests, which use multiple-choice and true-false formats. Also, it is a means to create authentic assessment challenges that resemble more closely what occurs in the world outside of the classroom.

Richard J. Stiggins, of the Northwest Regional Education Laboratory, defined these types of assessments, suggesting that persons could represent the assessment through any modality, and either alone or with a group. There are four components in Stiggins's definition that can occur at any point in the learning process, formally or informally: a reason for the assessment, a particular performance to be evaluated, exercises that elicit that performance, and systematic rating procedures.

It is clear that a transformation is occurring in assessment practices. Authentic assessment systems offer the ability to revolutionize how teachers, students, administrators, parents, and community members move forward to enhance the process of schooling.

Authentic assessment is a very large topic, and a growing body of knowledge is informing how to assess students more appropriately, how to work in teacher preparation programs with new forms of assessment, and how to enhance professionalism in evaluation processes with teachers and administrators. It is likely that as this movement toward authentic assessment grows in its sophistication and ease of implementation, it will begin to clarify the conversation about the best ways to assess students.

Authentic forms of assessment, even at this early point, can be trusted to provide different types of information from what is received currently in norm-referenced, multiple-choice testing. It can inform the teacher and student immediately about what steps to take next in the teaching-learning process, and it can be an active and sensitive means to work appropriately with students of varying needs who reside in the same classroom.

In the next chapter, we will begin to examine specific examples of how this authentic assessment process can be brought to life in the school setting.

Developing and Implementing an Authentic Assessment Program

Moving into authentic assessment and evaluation takes time! Teachers, administrators, parents, and students need time to work through the changes to create a more meaningful and authentic system of assessment. The process often involves changing our thinking about assessment and its relationship to instruction and student learning. As the changes occur, assessment and evaluation will become an integral part of the day-to-day instructional process, and students, teachers, parents, and administrators will be actively involved in the process.

Getting Started

The move to more authentic assessment and evaluation indicates a need for redefining the goals and methods of instruction. It will be important to investigate and discuss the changing beliefs and goals and to use these to form an updated guide for instruction. This provides opportunities for all involved to discuss what they believe the school experience should be, including the role of the teacher and the way students learn. The school community should reflect and consider if the current methods of instruction are effective in accomplishing its goals, and what assessment and evaluation shows about the needs of students.

As goals and philosophies change, assessment methods will need to be adjusted along with classroom practices. The school personnel should involve the community in developing new goals and in discussing how they will look in the classroom once they are implemented. When assessment is aligned with the goals and philosophy, assessment and evaluation become tools for guiding instruction. As the program is implemented, teachers will begin to use part of the class time to engage in assessment in more authentic situations as an integral part of instruction.

Organizing Records of Authentic Assessment

Anecdotal records of student performance can be filed together in a collection often referred to as a portfolio. Portfolios are more than folders filled with student work samples. A portfolio is a visual presentation of a student's accomplishments, capabilities, strengths, weaknesses, and progress over time. It provides an awareness of where the student has been, what steps were taken, and an idea of where the student is going. The portfolio will guide instruction and give insight into a student's decision-making and learning processes. The items that can be included in a portfolio are limitless, but if they are to be considered an authentic measure of a student's ability, they should fall into one of the following categories:

1. Represent authentic tasks done in different ways for a variety of purposes
2. Are ongoing and/or gathered over time
3. Sample a wide range of cognitive strategies
4. Provide for different developmental levels
5. Are unique to each child
6. Provide for collaborative reflection by student and teacher
7. Match and guide instruction
8. Emphasize what students know

Types of Portfolios

There are many different types of portfolios that teachers can consider. The most common include the working portfolio, the showcase portfolio, and the record-keeping portfolio.

The working portfolio is one in which the teacher and student assess and evaluate together. The students select samples to include in the portfolios that they believe show their learning and growth. Parents can add comments and the teacher can add samples and other records. The working portfolio presents the perspectives of the student, teacher, and parents to form a more accurate picture of the student's daily progress. It is important that the student feels ownership and that the teacher does not dominate the process of selecting and contributing pieces to the portfolio.

The showcase portfolio is similar to that of an artist's portfolio, which is prepared to show the artist's best work. This portfolio is limited to only the most outstanding pieces. Works in progress are not included. This type of portfolio motivates students to complete projects and other demonstrations of their best work and ability. In the showcase portfolio, the student usually has total ownership of the selections for the portfolio. This type of portfolio is not as useful for guiding instruction because the day-to-day performance is not included. When the portfolio is shared with parents, the parents are usually very impressed with their student's work, but they are not able to get a clear picture of their child's needs because only the best work is included.

The record-keeping portfolio is often used along with the showcase portfolio to contain a record of the completion of the necessary assessment and evaluation samples not chosen for the showcase portfolio but needed to document the completion of certain assignments.

What Do Portfolios Look Like?

There is no required look for portfolios. They can be packaged in a three-ring binder, scrapbook, box, file, accordion-type folder, or other system. The final decision should be determined by what the portfolios are going to contain and for how long a period of time they will be used. Because portfolios can provide an ongoing record of progress over time, they can include a very rich data bank. Although portfolios are most meaningful to the student and teacher as a guide to daily instruction and learning, it is also helpful to select samples to pass on to the teacher in the next semester, grade level, or class. Therefore, when selecting the format, the staff should consider if they want to provide enough room in the portfolio to contain each student's selected samples from the beginning to the end of the program, which, in some cases, could span years.

It is important that the size of the portfolio be managed easily if it is to be passed through the grade levels, classes, or program. The format must be workable for both teachers and students, and must be able to accommodate all kinds of samples, including tapes, computer disks, odd-sized papers, artwork, and so on. When determining the way to store gathered information, it is important to determine what the portfolio will contain, for what period of time, and if portfolios will be implemented schoolwide.

Filling the Portfolio

The teacher, student, and often the parent are all involved in contributing to the portfolio. As teachers observe and interact with the students, they collect samples, make anecdotal records, and note evidence of progress. Students also choose samples, reflect on their own work, and share their achievements with their peers and parents. For the portfolio system of authentic assessment to become effective, teachers, students, and parents need to become familiar with the methods of assessing, evaluating, and recording data. As students begin to share the responsibility for their own learning, they begin to understand how to help themselves learn.

Samples are usually selected from those developed primarily in the classroom that were a vital part of the ongoing instruction. When using this type of assessment, the teacher will ask more student questions, record their observations, and guide students in self-evaluation. The student and the teacher are involved with the ongoing development of the portfolio. Student self-evaluation is an important component of portfolio assessment and evaluation. Parents are involved through their comments, suggestions, and classroom visits.

Contents of Portfolios

The following is a description of the general types of contents a portfolio can include.

Process Samples or Works in Progress. These uncompleted items show how students go through the process of completing a task. They enable the reader to understand more clearly how students think and what strategies and procedures they use.

Product Samples. These items are the finished, revised, edited works that show students' strengths and achievements. Large projects, oral reports, or skits can be included in the form of audio- or videotapes or snapshots.

Teacher Observations or Assessment Data. This is information gathered through teachers' notes of observations, assessments, and a variety of other evaluation strategies.

Parent Comments. This section includes notes from parents after reviewing the contents of the portfolio.

A portfolio for language arts could include a reading development checklist, writing samples, a list of books read by the student, a test of reading comprehension, a list of topics and authors the student enjoys, audiotapes and charts indicating reading fluency, summaries of interviews with the students about their attitudes on reading and writing, teacher anecdotal records, the student's self-evaluation of his or her own reading and writing ability, and parent comments.

Menu-Driven Portfolios

When collecting samples and information for the portfolio, it is important that there be a balance between process and product samples as well as a wide variety of materials to give a broad view of the students' abilities and evidence that they have achieved the goals. To accomplish this end, teachers often prepare a menu that acts as a table of contents guiding the selection of materials for the portfolio. This menu can include some items that are very general and others that are specific. Some items on the menu could be required, whereas others are optional or enable students to choose from a list of options. The menu could include samples from across the curricula, teacher observations, inventories or other forms, test results, and even a category for wild card items.

Wild card selections provide students with autonomy, accommodate a wide variety of learning styles, and encourage creativity and variety. A wild card section is a place for students to include other items that are not on the menu but are products of which they are particularly proud. This section could include cassettes, videos, or photos of presentations or exhibits, as well as letters from peers or community members documenting or evaluating contributions the student has made. If projects won't fit in the portfolio or were group efforts, a photograph of the event or product can be included along with the student's reflective writing about the activity that states what was learned in the process of developing the project. Each sample should be dated and include an anecdotal note from the student explaining why it was selected, where it was collected, what it shows about his or her progress, and other data.

Surveys, comments, or evaluations from parents are also an important part of the portfolio. They not only provide the teacher with valuable information, but also give parents an excellent opportunity to become involved in their student's education.

Owing to time constraints and the difficulty of storing and handling masses of information, the old adage of promoting quality over quantity would apply when preparing a menu or selecting materials for a broad-based assessment portfolio.

Considerations for the Teacher's Section

Teacher observations and measures could be included in another section. Daily and ongoing observations of students are at the heart of collecting and building portfolios. By observing the student while he or she is participating in a lesson, working with an adult or other students, or working independently, the teacher gains important information about the processes students use to learn. Anecdotal records are objective—they report rather than evaluate or interpret. As students' observations are recorded, their names can be marked off on a checklist to make sure that all students are observed. It is surprising what a short time it can take to write a brief note to every student in the class.

Additional materials that can be added to the teacher anecdotal record section of the portfolio include a running record, a retelling, progress checks, teacher-made tests, conference records, and a final report. A brief overview of these items is included in the following paragraphs.

The *reading record* is a record made on the run; it was originally used as a part of the Reading Recovery Program.

Retelling is the process of students retelling what they just read either verbally or in writing, giving the teacher an opportunity to evaluate comprehension, sequencing of ideas, and ability to reconstruct the text. When the retelling is written, it also provides the teacher an opportunity to evaluate progress in spelling, grammar, and writing, as well as comprehension skills.

The *progress check* is an open format that gives children the opportunity to share what they have learned. It is not guided with a list of questions from the teacher.

When designing *teacher-made tests*, it is important to include opportunities for students to demonstrate their understanding regardless of the way they learn.

The *conference records* are summaries of the discussion and decisions made jointly by students and teachers during regularly held conferences. Conference records should be made every week or two, as the teacher confers with each student. If the teacher has a student for more than one subject, conference records for each subject can be color coded.

The *final report* is a summary of the student's growth throughout the year or course. This will be an important document for the student's next teacher. This provides the teacher with an opportunity for building a long-term view of the student's development and overall progress. The key factors that should be included are the student's learning strategies, learning preferences, attitudes, and work and study habits. The summary should emphasize what the student can do and focus on the changes and growth the student has made.

Inventories also can be considered for inclusion in the teacher's section of the portfolio. These could include interest, reading, or writing lists.

Preventing Biases

It is important to remember that using alternative assessment and a variety of measures does not guarantee the collection of accurate, unbiased data. When assessment content is oriented to topics and culture unfamiliar to the student, or it seeks responses that are based on background knowledge achieved by those with an economic and educational advantage, the results will be biased.

The Role of Standardized and Authentic Assessment

An effort must be made to protect teachers and students from the loss of valuable instructional time because of overtesting. The quality of the data gained from all forms of assessment must be questioned and evaluated constantly, and it must be determined if other methods of evaluation provide teachers with more valuable information that is more aligned with their instructional program. Standardized tests are a single measure of an individual performance and are therefore misleading when they are used as the sole basis for determining how a student will perform in future educational settings or as an employee in a workplace.

Currently, the results of standardized tests are valued as an accountability measure. As the move toward more authentic assessment progresses in the classroom, the nature and design of large-scale standardized testing is changing to enhance the relationship of outcomes to instruction. However, time may be a critical factor because large-scale testing involves more teachers in the development, review, and scoring of items. Therefore, it is important that teachers and administrators share information about the purpose and use of testing with parents and communities so that only those assessments that provide valid and useful information will be used.

It seems that both forms of assessment will be available for some time to come. Therefore, the results of formal and informal authentic assessment can be used to form a comprehensive picture of a student's overall progress.

The Teacher's Role in Authentic Assessment

The teacher's shift to authentic assessment will not be a magical transformation that takes place overnight. The changes in the teacher's roles and responsibilities, going from the teacher-centered classroom to one focused on student learning, requires the integration of new instructional and assessment skills, which can best be accomplished over time.

These changes require teachers to know how to formulate learning goals, plan instruction to include assessment and documentation of learning, and develop methods to store, grade, disseminate, and interpret authentic assessments of learning. To begin using authentic assessment measures, teachers must address several issues and questions: What will be the goals for learning? What will be the authentic assessment tasks that best measure the goals? What type of management system will be used in organizing the authentic assessment tasks? How will authentic assessment be integrated into instruction? What will be the criteria and process for selection of materials to be placed into the portfolios? How will they be evaluated? Who will review them? What will be done with the completed portfolios?

Establishing the Goals for Assessment

For each content area, major topic, or concept, the teacher will need to identify precisely the meaningful student outcomes or goals for learning. Formulating clear goals that reflect the major outcomes of instruction is an important first step to implementing an authentic assessment system. These goals will help determine the best method of instruction as well as assist in the selection of the most appropriate assessment activity, one that will enable students to demonstrate achievement of the goal. Without clear goals, there is a tendency to select things that are easy to measure that are not meaningful to students, instead of asking what is important and will measure significant student learning and the ability to apply it to real-life situations.

Selecting the Authentic Assessment Activities

There is wide variation among teachers in selecting authentic assessment tasks in the classroom. In Chapter 2, the criteria for selecting items that are considered authentic tasks, the most common types of portfolios (working, showcase, and record-keeping), and possible contents for portfolios were described. Teachers will need to explore to find out which types of portfolios and formats, or combinations of the two, work best for them, their students, and the parents. Teachers will need to determine if the contents of the portfolio will be listed in a menu. Will there be a section in the portfolio for students, teacher, and parents? If so, will there be required or suggested items? Will there be a section for various content areas, or will there be a list of learning outcomes and a wide variety of suggested ways in which students can demonstrate their learning?

The identification of which authentic assessment measures to include can be simplified if teachers select those that capitalize on the actual work of the classroom and those that enhance teacher, student, and parent involvement in determining if learning goals have been met while meeting a majority of the other accountability needs and concerns.

The value of the assessment tasks will depend on the teacher's ability to plan complex and significant tasks that enable students to use prior knowledge, recent learning, and relevant skills. It is important that students be invited to solve meaningful and realistic problems that assess progress on learning outcomes. The assessment task must be engaging and of interest to students if the teacher is to assume that it represents their best work.

The contents of the portfolio can vary greatly from teacher to teacher because of the wide selection of possible tasks and activities that can be used to reflect the student's achievements, and because the selection of activities is based on each individual teacher's goals and purpose for using portfolios. A few of the many items that can be considered for authentic assessment tasks to demonstrate learning are included in the following list.

Audiotapes
Anecdotal records (student or teacher)
Book reports (including a wide variety of options)
Computer disks
Computer shows
Conference records (student-teacher-parent or student-teacher)
Current events
Drawings and diagrams
Favorite authors
Field trip reports
"Great Discoveries" page
Interviews
Inventories (interest, reading, etc.)
Investigations
Journals
List of books read by the student
Models with descriptions
Murals
News items with the student's commentary and analysis
Open-ended problems
Parent comments
Photographs of collections
Problem-solving activities

Progress reports
Project reports, summaries, or videos
Projects, pictures, or videos of entries in a competition
Proposals for experiments or research
Reading development checklist
Reading logs or records
Research lab investigations
Research papers
Running reading records
Self-evaluations
Simulations
Skits and puppet shows
Student's responses to teacher-presented "Big Ideas" or questions
Student-selected best work
Student's self-evaluations
Teacher observations
Teacher-student conference summaries
Testing (a test of reading comprehension, etc.)
Time lines
Writing samples: mechanical (simple recall), transactional (note-taking and summaries), expressive (one's thoughts and feel-ings), and/or creative (using one's imagination)
Videotapes
Work samples

Changing the Portfolio Contents

As measures of performance are developed, it is important for teachers to understand that they exist to strengthen their own as well as the student's judgment of learning and provide them both with helpful information in planning the next learning sequence. Teachers often revise and refine their portfolio from year to year, adjusting the content of the portfolio so that activities provide the greatest benefit to their classroom teaching and student learning. Changing the requirements also comes about because students or teachers have grown beyond the original scheme and need more challenging experiences. However, if teachers and students are satisfied with the format, the contents of the portfolio do not need to be altered.

Selecting a Management System for the Portfolio System

The teacher will need to determine how the authentic assessment measures will be stored during the year. The decision will be determined by how many and what type of authentic assessment measures will be assigned, how long they will be used to contain the information, and where they will be stored. If it is a school- or departmentwide program, these decisions will need to be made with other teachers.

The teacher will determine how and when materials can be placed into the portfolio and what procedure is to be followed before placing them there. It will also need to be determined who decides what material is passed on at the end of the term and how, when, and where this material is delivered or stored. It will be important to clarify who will keep the remaining materials at the end of the term or year. Generally, they are returned to the student.

Integrating Authentic Assessment Into Instruction

One of the most frequently voiced concerns raised by teachers interested in authentic assessment is the question, Where do I find the time? Given that the curriculum is being revised regularly by the addition of new programs, textbooks, and issues that schools are pressured to address, it is no wonder that this concern is expressed when it looks as if something else may be added to an already overcrowded school day.

It is important for teachers to understand that authentic assessment is not something that is added to the long list of teacher responsibilities or record-keeping responsibilities. Authentic assessment does not demand more time from teachers during or beyond the school day. Authentic assessment is done instead of some of the current teaching and record-keeping activities. Using an authentic assessment process requires that teachers reevaluate the instructional and assessment decisions they make within the school day, discontinue some of them, and replace them with others.

Instead of lecturing during the entire period and grading papers alone at the end of the day after the students have left, the teacher in a meaning-centered, activity-based classroom integrates assessment and evaluation activities into instruction and conducts assessment with students during the class period. Many teachers are finding that planning appropriate instruction, both daily and long range, is facilitated when assessment is an integral part of the curriculum. This in-process assessment and evaluation of the products of learning informs teachers of what students know, can do, and are ready to learn. These ongoing activities will enable the teacher to have more immediate feedback on their students' abilities and help them determine where the learners are in the process of meeting the goals.

Most students have a great interest in their peers and can learn a tremendous amount from each other by working together on projects or sharing their work. Authentic assessment lends itself to cooperative learning or other forms of group work. Students put forth a greater effort because they want to share something they deem valuable with the group. When students review their portfolios, they begin to feel the value and ownership of their work; when this occurs, the focus of education is where it belongs—with the student. Introducing concepts through manipulatives and group work allows students to investigate ideas more thoroughly and retain them longer than does memorizing rules by themselves. However, teachers need to make sure that there are no shortcuts that defeat the purposes of authentic assessment, such as parents or siblings doing a student's work; group work that totally replaces individual initiative; or computers that provide a slick finish, but not necessarily better substance.

When using authentic assessment, teachers schedule specific times during the class session to observe students, collect samples and data, and confer with students to evaluate. Evaluation becomes a collaborative effort between the teacher and student and is an integral part of the daily learning activities. As teachers observe the learning process, select samples, make anecdotal records, and note other evidence of progress, students also complete activities, choose samples, reflect on their work, and share their achievements with other students or the teacher. Often the best assessments are a natural outgrowth of a teaching sequence that integrates assessment within the instructional process and weaves planning and teaching with evaluation.

Before the teacher begins integrating assessment with instruction, it is imperative that they have selected their learning goals and then consider the various meaning-centered assessment procedures that can be integrated with instruction.

Integrating Problem-Solving and Communication Skills

Problem solving is not something that can be added to the curriculum as a 2-week unit of study. It needs to be integrated into the instruction. The emphasis of instruction needs to be moved from the memorization of isolated facts to more complex tasks that cause students to integrate, apply, and analyze the facts.

As with the process approach to writing instruction, which has been in place for more than a decade, students develop their ideas through many drafts, with less emphasis on the end product and more emphasis on the learning and thinking process. The use of the process approach encourages students to continually refine their ideas and encourages teachers to go beyond the level of recall and comprehension and include a broad range of more complex thinking activities.

The thrust of instruction needs to go beyond just getting the right answer. It encompasses communicating how the student solved the problem, why decisions were made along the way, and what connections were made with other leanings during the problem-solving process. This will mean involving students in many problem-solving situations in lieu of drill and worksheet activities and assessing all steps of their work using problem-solving and communication criteria. Students will begin to be able to assess their own work and focus on all aspects of problems. Problem solving becomes an integral part of the curriculum. By introducing concepts through manipulatives and group work, students are able to investigate their own and other students' ideas more thoroughly.

The portfolio can include student work on authentic assessment tasks that are used to assess problem-solving and communication skills using seven criteria:

- Understanding the task
- Applying a problem-solving strategy
- Making decisions
- Verifying the solution
- Making connections
- Using rich language
- Using effective representations.

Teachers must understand that problem solving involves more than simply getting the answer. It encompasses communicating through language and representations how the student solved the problem, why certain decisions were made along the way, and what connections the student was able to make during the problem-solving process. This will necessitate involving students in many problem-solving situations and assessing the work using problem-solving and communication criteria.

Addressing students' questions and enduring issues and ideas gets students actively engaged in problem solving and a variety of experiential learning opportunities. Students need to be given the opportunity to integrate problem solving and technology, and interdisciplinary and real-world applications. Greater emphasis on understanding, hands-on learning experiences, and collaborative group work will help students use the tools, techniques, and ideas to develop their understanding of the world around them and to communicate solutions to real-life problems. Hands-on materials and activities, including the use of diagrams, graphs, calculators, and computers, help students learn to solve problems they will face in the real world.

The integration of problem solving requires teachers to provide a classroom environment that encourages problem solving and models the curiosity, flexibility, and reflection to confront problems that we have no ready means to solve. Students need to become risk takers who persevere through challenging and engaging tasks. When portfolios are coupled with this type of instruction, students are curious, flexible in their approach, and able to reflect on their growth.

Authentic assessment tasks require students to demonstrate their understanding of concepts and processes that integrate their learning in varied ways, reinforcing the highest goals of instruction. Assessment tasks must be patterned after instruction and must emphasize production, creation, and performance. Assessment tasks should be multidimensional in the skills assessed, multisensory in stimuli presented, and multimodal in response formats. Authentic assessment tasks fit these criteria.

The Teacher's Role in Guiding the Learning

The root of the word *assessment* means to sit with a learner and seek to be sure that a student's responses really mean what they seem to mean. Assessment for teachers is successful only to the extent that it can be used to improve instruction for students. Research has found that teachers' informal observations of students engaged in meaningful activities and intuitions about children's needs are far more useful than scores from formal tests for guiding instruction.

Notes on classroom discussions, enthusiasm for or avoidance of certain authors or topics, spontaneous self-corrections of miscues, puzzled looks or questions asked in class, informal interviews, and the quality of daily work are all found in the teacher's anecdotal records. All of these informal observations provide teachers with continual feedback and guidance on students' development. Along with the other authentic assessment measures, the teacher's anecdotal records can augment and systematize the collections of information that will be helpful in making sound instructional decisions.

Authentic assessment involves continuous monitoring and diagnosing of students' progress of learning and completed work. Knowing what to look for, when to look, and being able to identify what they see is central for teachers who want to succeed in a class-room focused on the authentic assessment of student learning.

Standardized assessment conducted solely in the form of paper-pencil tests reduces children's efforts as learners to numbers that indicate how many questions each child answered correctly on the day the test was given. These snapshot assessments miss fundamental qualities of human effort and possibility. Subtleties of thought, patterns of effort, and areas of interest or wonder that can promote further learning help us plan effective next steps or provide evidence of emerging self-awareness. If we rely solely on standardized or paper-pencil tests to assess student learning, we have a limited knowledge and view of learning. By using their knowledge of students, teachers can note subtle patterns and continuities that persons outside the classroom cannot observe. It works against using easy labels and prescriptions based on one-time events and gives us a broader and longer term account of the child.

Teachers can identify important characteristic patterns in interests and strengths, choices, ways of perceiving and constructing order, gaps in learning, and modes of thinking and learning. The teacher's records provide an important opportunity to reconceive the relationship between schools and parents. They promote the collaboration between home and school based on a mutual effort to identify and support children's interests and strengths. The teacher's descriptive records keep assessment close to the ongoing classroom activities, and the knowledge they yield is of great benefit to children, parents, and other educators.

Some teachers keep notes on conference sheets stapled to the inside of each student's portfolio or folder so that they are available to students at all times. Other teachers keep one notebook with a separate page for each student or maintain a checklist of important strategies or behaviors that can be marked along with anecdotal notes or other information not listed that is important to record. This system often develops from a teacher's initial jottings. To get started, the teacher needs to select a system of taking anecdotal notes that is narrow in scope, manageable, and not so cumbersome that it is abandoned after a few weeks of use. Gradually, teachers will develop their own system or checklist that is most workable for their goals and purposes. Other teachers select a checklist or system, or adapt one developed by a colleague. Some teachers modify and combine several systems to suit their purposes. These anecdotal records serve as an ongoing record to use with parents during conference time.

Evaluating Student Work

Evaluation begins as students go through the process of selecting, revising, and reflecting. It should be an ongoing procedure that is linked to the purpose of the project and the portfolio rather than a prescribed formal assessment process.

A rubric is a set of criteria that is often used as a form of evaluation because it provides teachers, students, and parents with a description of different levels of performance in terms of what students are able to do and assigns a value to each of the levels. Rubrics are used to score portfolios and assess writing and class, school, or district performance.

Rubrics can be used as advanced organizers at the beginning of a unit of instruction so that learning expectations are known and understood up front. Rubrics can be used to evaluate process as well as content. They might be a global, analytic, or holistic method. Rubrics should have enough detail so that there are no questions as to how well the activity was done. They can be created by teachers, students and teachers or students working together, or by a district or state committee or other interested parties. Steps for developing a rubric include the following:

Step 1. Start by making a list of the most important components or expectations of a learning activity. These might include the process, content, mechanics, presentation, variety and number of source materials, neatness, and other factors that are important to the activity.

Step 2. Determine the criteria you will use for a scale. It might start with Excellent or 5 and scale down. Write a description or number for as many additional categories as you desire. Rubrics using more than six criteria descriptions are more difficult to use.

Step 3. Write a description of the performance expected for each criterion. Include the components you previously identified as important to this activity in your description of performance at each level. Some criteria on the scale may have more components assigned to them than others.

Rubrics for writing will vary for the different styles of writing. They include written descriptions of students' performance for each scoring level and could include an evaluation of a student's ability to focus and take a position, their organization, coherence in writing, depth or elaboration, clarity, word choice, and sentence variety. Rubrics for different assignments within a subject area may also vary to match the expectations of the particular assignment or individual student. A sample of a rubric is shown below.

Score 4 = Fully accomplishes the purpose of the task. Shows full grasp and use of the central ideas using a combination of skills.

Score 3 = Substantially accomplishes the purpose of the task. Shows essential grasp of the central idea. In general, the work communicates the student's thinking.

Score 2 = Partially accomplishes the purpose of the task. Shows partial but limited grasp of the idea. Recorded work may be incomplete, misdirected, or not clearly presented.

Score 1 = Little or no progress toward accomplishing the task. Shows little or no grasp of the central idea. Work is hard to understand.

Rubrics can be organized around a number of equally weighted factors, with a graduated criterion for each factor. To develop this type of rubric, list equally weighted factors and three to four criteria with a description for each criterion for every factor. Each criterion should be weighted for each of the factors. If one factor is determined to be more important, it can be weighted higher. The criteria for other, less important factors can be given less weight. This type of rubric can include such factors as making personal, historical, or cultural connections; taking risks; challenging the text; applying prior experiences; making predictions or speculating; elaborating an emotional response; and reflecting on and using the complexities of language.

Rubrics are a useful means of evaluating student performance in an integrated, meaning-centered curriculum. To succeed in the 21st century, students will need both the structure for security and the freedom to try new things. Rubrics provide even clearer expectations and directions than the letter grade system. They allow students to be involved in planning how they will demonstrate their learning, which increases involvement, motivation, buy-in, interest, and most important, learning.

If teachers develop consistent scoring methods on the same rubric within a district, state, or nation and align them to the instructional goals, they will gain the ability to compare student performances across large groups. In this way, teachers can provide the hard numbers that will help solve accountability problems. As educators work with rubrics, they are becoming skilled at gathering trustworthy data and developing the ability to conduct rigorous, defensible analyses that might enable them to use authentic assessment to meet more than classroom instructional assessment and accountability needs.

The Issue of Grading

To grade or not to grade should not be the question! The purpose of using portfolios is the key to determining whether they should be graded. If the teacher has replaced traditional instruction with a process approach, including debates, learning logs, interviews, mock trials, journals, research reports, and portfolios, a process-focused assessment naturally follows. This could include a student-led conference, a written summary prepared by both the student and teacher, or a number of other options.

If a teacher decided to use portfolios to motivate students as learners, he or she might choose to leave the portfolios out of the grading loop. In contrast, a teacher might believe that the parents or students will respond more readily to a letter grade and that omitting grades limits the motivational power of the portfolio. They may use cumulative points from the rubric scoring to determine a grading scale.

How to Start

When teachers implement authentic assessment, it is advisable to begin with a few topics or one subject, develop goals for those topics, and then develop suitable activities to measure the goals that can be integrated into the instructional process. In this way, the teacher will have a manageable system and not feel overwhelmed while they are developing their abilities as a learner-centered, classroom-based evaluator.

Developing an accurate and complete picture of a student's progress, strengths, and needs will require a variety of measures. It is important that teachers feel free to develop a 2- or 3-year plan in which to expand and adapt the concept of authentic assessment in ways that will better meet their instructional goals and the needs of their students and the school community. Student work is often evaluated using a rubric.

This scoring guide is designed to evaluate a student's performance, often within a specific curricular area. When designing a rubric, the first step is to select the components to be addressed or measured by the rubric. For example, a rubric for the area of writing could include components that measure organization of ideas, word choice, sentence structure, and mechanics. Once these components have been identified, a rating scale is selected, typically from 0 to 4 or 0 to 6, with the largest number indicating an outstanding score. Finally, the teacher (or teacher and students) writes the criteria describing the performance for each of the components being evaluated for each number. When scoring with a rubric, the description that best matches the student's work is selected and the corresponding number becomes the score.

The reason for using rubric scoring is to help students and teachers clarify the criteria and to involve students in self-evaluation. Including students in the designing of the rubric helps them develop the vocabulary and clarify their understanding of the goals and expectations for a variety of assignments in different subject areas. It enables students to take more responsibility for their learning and is far more specific and meaningful than a letter grade.

Involving Students, Parents, and the Community in the Learning Process

A uthentic assessment is a positive and dynamic form of evaluation. It is a system that documents what students can do; promotes the collaboration of teacher, student, and parent in the learning process; and places the ownership of learning on the student. But how should teachers and the administration proceed with students, parents, and the community when implementing authentic assessment? This chapter reviews some possible ways to prepare the students, inform the parents and community, and involve them in the process.

Preparing the Students

When implementing authentic assessment, teachers should evaluate students' ability to answer open-ended, interpretive, applied, and higher order essay questions. In an ongoing process, they need to provide the appropriate instruction to help students gain the skills necessary to respond to these questions. Teachers should be using instructional time for meaning-centered activities as well as teacher-directed lessons to teach their students content and the skills necessary to ensure success with performance measures.

Students who have had a steady diet of recall-oriented, objective questions such as multiple-choice, true or false, matching, fill-in-the-blank, and so on will often leave answers blank or incomplete, or else they will give such general answers that the answers are meaningless because the students have had little experience in answering interpretive, application, and higher order questions. When this happens, teachers wonder if students are of such low ability that they cannot respond to higher order thinking questions, or they assume that their teaching was not effective. Teachers may abandon using more authentic assessment measures on the basis of poor initial results because they do not understand the cause. Therefore, one of the first steps is to assess students' preparedness to respond to the new level of questioning and thinking, and to take class time to teach and perfect the skills and techniques to think at higher levels.

Teaching Students to Think

Most students who have primarily experienced lower level questioning do not know how to respond to verbal or written questions containing verbs such as *define, list, state, compare, summarize, analyze,* and *evaluate.* They are often unable to identify the essential directive verbs in the question, are not sure what they mean, and cannot translate them into an appropriate answer without undergoing instruction. It is important to remember that instruction on these skills needs to take place when teaching all subject areas, not just during English and language arts. These skills are the most meaningful when they are tied to content. Leaving it to only the English or science teacher will not achieve the desired results. Teaching and practicing these skills daily in all subjects will reinforce student learning and guide students in developing the skills they need to communicate effectively their knowledge in any area.

Long exposure to standardized and multiple-choice tests has conditioned students to read a question quickly and select the first answer that comes to mind. Many students have been conditioned not to think too deeply or to read too carefully because if they do, they are sure to read too much into the question and get it wrong. When higher levels of thinking are required, these attitudes are incorrect. Through effective use of oral questioning strategies, such as prompting and probing, teachers can get many students to verbally articulate a process, concept, or procedure by answering a multitude of "What if?" questions. However, without teaching the needed skills or providing oral or written guidance, students often cannot translate their knowledge into written work required on essay tests or lab reports, and ultimately in the world of work.

Responding With Complete Answers

Often students have formed the habit of viewing the teacher as their only audience for their oral classroom responses, and they omit key information, assuming the teacher already knows the material. By doing so, they omit vital background information and necessary supporting details in their written responses. Without assessing and, if necessary, preteaching the needed skills, teachers cannot be certain that these new evaluative tools are truly reflective of the capabilities and knowledge of their students.

To help students learn the skills to correctly respond to higher order thinking questions, teachers will need to develop some exercises using materials directly related to the subject matter that the class is studying at the time. From existing activity or lab sheets, tests, and quizzes, teachers can create a series of exercises focusing on the identification of the key words in each question. These are the words that appear frequently in written questions that students need to be able to identify, define, and understand if they are to answer the questions. When working with them, teachers can use existing questions to identify guiding words such as *compare, evaluate, judge, assess, decide, rank, infer, interpret, figure out, account for, explain,* and so on.

Students, working alone or in small groups, should be given exercises in which they are asked to read through a question first and then underline the key words. Teachers should help students define each of the key words in terms of what they should do: When comparing, students should discuss how things are alike and how they are different. When evaluating, judging, assessing, deciding, and ranking, students should make judgments of what is correct or incorrect according to the information they have. When inferring, interpreting, figuring out, accounting for, or explaining, students should know that they need to go beyond the data provided and give unique explanations or causes for events described in the question.

Planning Practice Experiences for the Class

A classroom activity that provides effective practice involves asking small groups to review examples of students' answers that they have prepared that are insufficient or too general. If actual examples of student's responses are used, it is critical that they be altered by the teacher to the degree that no students, not even the author, recognize the source of the example. This will help to preserve students' self-esteem and dignity. Identifying students as bad examples when they are learning a new and difficult skill will snuff out any desire for them to attempt to learn other new skills, and will certainly dampen their motivation for school and their respect for the adult in charge.

It is helpful if students are encouraged to verbalize their thought processes as they answer, or as they explain to the other students how they arrived at their answer. It is also helpful to have students pretend that they are addressing their answer to someone with no knowledge of the topic. In this way, they develop the skill of including every appropriate point.

Helping Students Evaluate Their Own Learning

When implementing an authentic assessment system, students will also need to develop the skills to evaluate their own work. When they do not know the elements that make a work excellent, they cannot determine the quality of their own work or why one product is better than another. The skills of self-evaluation need to be taught and nurtured. Students' ability to understand their work in relation to other work they have completed or the work of others, build on their strengths, see new possibilities and challenges in their work, and become eager lifelong learners all depends on their capacity to step back from their work and consider it carefully, drawing insights and ideas about themselves as learners. This kind of mindful capacity of students to reflect, judge, and refine their own work and efforts before, during, and after the process is one of the goals of authentic assessment.

The movement toward a more authentic and meaningful assessment has uncovered just how much help students need in order to learn how to evaluate their own work. It takes time for students to develop the ability to reflect on the merits of their work and to gain confidence in becoming a critic. When students are allowed to decide which works belong in their portfolios without training, their reasons for their decisions are casual: "I'm choosing this one because it is about the Romans." "This is my longest one." "I am putting this in because the teacher gave me an 'A' on this research paper." Developing the skill of self-evaluation is a critical step in building a successful authentic assessment system. The skills will then need to be supported and expanded if the program is to continue successfully over time.

Activities to Learn Self-Evaluation

During the learning phase, teachers should draft a sample that includes illustrations of strengths and weaknesses or take examples from several students' work and alter them significantly so that even those students do not recognize portions of the final product as their work. Evaluating a sample that does not represent any single person's initial efforts enables the other students to express openly their beginning understandings of evaluation, questions, and thoughts without the fear of embarrassing their classmates.

To foster initial success, the process of evaluation should be practiced with the whole class or in small groups of students working together, so that students can benefit from the thinking of other students, which lowers the level of difficulty of a new process. After students have grasped the process and are able to assess the samples of work with ease in whole class or small group settings, they can begin working in pairs to assess their own work. Once students understand the elements that denote quality work, they are better able to self-evaluate before, during, and after completion of an assignment, making needed modifications in their own work as it is completed and making better decisions when choosing work to place in their portfolio.

Although forms are often used to help guide students' evaluation of their own learning, students should be encouraged to reflect on their learning by writing about their reactions. This will provide more information about their attitudes, styles of learning, and self-concept. Questions that students should be able to respond to include:

- Why did they choose the sample for their portfolio?
- What do they think is especially good about the work?
- How does the sample compare with other samples they have completed?
- What growth do they see?
- Which piece do they think is the best and what makes it the best?
- What was helpful and what was difficult?
- What could make it better?
- How has their work has changed over the year?

Once this questioning has been modeled for students and practiced by the whole class and small groups, students are better able to question themselves in a similar manner and approach the task of self-evaluation with greater confidence and ability.

When students become skilled in the process of self-evaluation, they might keep logs as a way of tracking their daily progress, reporting and describing what they did, and noting comments and thoughts about various decisions and choices they make as learners. Once they are accomplished in the process, students will be confident in their abilities and will willingly share their work, engage in lively classroom discussions, ponder possible strategies for improving their work, make judgments and distinctions about what they like and dislike, and determine what makes some work powerful and riveting and other works dull and uninteresting.

When students become confident in self-evaluation, they will participate in lengthy peer-response sessions and interviews, share and hone their skills for making thoughtful judgments, and pose challenging questions about the process as well as the completed product. Students will develop a sense of their growth and learning over time as they reflect on their past work.

Students' ability to thoughtfully tackle complex tasks grows out of their capacity to judge and refine their work and efforts over a period of time. Developing students' abilities to self-assess and reflect provides critical information on the complex and often invisible dimensions of student learning and provides a critical portion of the total assessment picture. Of course, the teachers' and parents' perceptions of the students' efforts are equally important to completing the assessment process.

Once students are proficient at self-evaluation, diverse learning opportunities will become even more powerful learning experiences. Students should be continually challenged to tackle project work regularly and frequently and to explore many aspects of a discipline. They should judge their own work again and again as it is in progress, completed, or in relation to earlier or later works. Students should collaborate and converse with other students as a critical element in the process of becoming a thinking and active learner.

Many opportunities should be provided for students to discuss, hear, and learn from others' perceptions. Students need to be challenged to reflect on the intent and purpose of their work and encouraged to identify a real audience for their work beyond the classroom teacher. Students begin to grasp the concept of what it means to get better when they assess their learning and development over time—not just at the end of a year or course, but across the weeks, months, and even years of their academic and lifetime learning careers. The process of performance assessment first must be learned by the teacher, student, and parent, and then they will make use of feedback and reflection to provoke further learning.

Involving Parents and the Community

In an effective authentic assessment program, parents become partners with teachers and students, and parents are seen as a rich source of information. Diverse efforts should be made to inform and include parents in all aspects of the authentic assessment program. Parents can be invited to attend a special forum offered at different times during the day and in the evening to find out about authentic assessment, how it is different than what was done before, how and what the process measures, how their student's work is scored, and how their progress will be reported. Information should be included about different types of assessment efforts, and samples of authentic tasks, scoring rubrics, and actual portfolios should be available.

The presentation should include a description of the key characteristics of an assessment system based on student performance. These might include an overview of the following performance assessment components:

- It is reflective of what students know about what they are learning.
- It is centered in the classroom.
- It is compatible with curricular and instructional goals.
- It is qualitative as well as quantitative.
- It is multidimensional and leads to a profile of growth and progress over time.
- It is focused on learning and developed by the primary stakeholders: the teacher, student, and parent.
- It is useful in guiding decisions for next steps in the instructional process.

Time should be allowed for questions and discussion. If possible, it will be important to provide child care. Videos of the presentation can be made available to local video stores, the library, or in the front office of the school so that parents and members of the community and board of education who were unable to attend the meetings can view it at home. The goal of the meetings should be to help parents understand that the process of learning and the construction of meaning is the purpose of instruction.

Parents Share in Planning Outcomes

There are many ways to invite parents to share in the authentic assessment process. At the beginning of the school year, the teacher can send home a letter asking parents to take a few moments to share some knowledge of their student's strengths and weaknesses; their interests; other information they feel would be important for the teacher to know; and their wishes, hopes, and dreams for their student during the upcoming school year.

Most parents will labor over their responses, caring about the student's welfare and trusting that the teacher who asks does too. The parents' response can serve as a focus for conferences and progress reports.

Parent Participation Throughout the Year

Parents should have many opportunities to attend seminars, meet with teachers, join ongoing curriculum or assessment committees, and read brochures and newsletter reports about performance assessment. Specific examples of portfolios, seminars, and videos about performance assessment also can be made available to parent groups.

Through training, parents can be helped to understand how teachers select tasks and set standards that enable them to guide the instructional process. It is also helpful if information is sent home to keep parents up-to-date throughout the year about the implementation of the authentic assessment program. The implications of using portfolios and other authentic measures of assessment can be discussed and parents can be invited to an unofficial practice scoring session. Teachers can share their results with the parents and the community and explain how they plan to respond in terms of adjustments to the curriculum, instruction, or to the assessment system itself.

How Can I Help My Student?

Parents often ask, How can I help my student succeed in performance assessment? There are many things parents can do to support their children's education.

- Talk with your students about their studies, homework, and what they did at school.
- Listen to your students as they talk about what they have read or what projects they are working on for their portfolio.

- Have a family reading time when you read the newspaper, a magazine, or a book, and your students read their own book or magazine.
- Encourage your students to write things such as shopping lists, thank you notes, short stories, recipes, and personal journals.
- Set limits on the amount of time your students can watch television, and try to watch and discuss programs with them.
- Take your students to the library regularly and help them select their books.
- Check with your students about homework and make sure that assignments are completed.
- Have your students explain how they go about solving problems from daily life.
- Ask questions as you help your students go through the process of solving problems, playing games, watching television, or making a favorite recipe.
- Show your students how they can use the skills or information they have told you they are studying in school in everyday situations.
- Ask for and attend student-parent-teacher conferences to find out what your students are achieving and what they need to do to improve.

It is critical that parents get involved. Their support will make a significant difference in their students' achievement.

Including the Community in Performance Assessment

Educating community groups that are interested in and responsible for education must parallel the teachers' experiences in the classroom. If portfolio assessment is to deliver on its great potential, educating parents and community leaders fully about its elements and its usefulness is as important as training teachers.

The larger community also can become involved in reviewing portfolios. Students can present their portfolios to a group of four or five community members, including the student's teacher or advisor, a staff member, another student, and a person of the student's choice. Students may select a parent or a member of the community. Students can be asked to present, defend, and answer questions about their portfolio as a culminating experience for a course, school year, or part of the graduation requirements. Members of the audience and the students talk directly to each other, and these conversations encourage students to do additional reflection on their work.

Portfolios also can be shared at school board meetings. School board members, who are used to looking at learning in terms of test scores, cannot see the learning itself. Having five or six students share what they learned from their portfolio will be very meaningful to board members. This also could be done for service organizations in the community. Having teachers share what their students are learning, explain how they base teaching decisions on performance assessment, and illustrate those generalizations with actual portfolios, is very meaningful. This same type of presentation can be included in the parent information meeting discussed earlier. A video of this presentation can be made available free of charge at the local video store or library for checkout to parents and community members so they can watch at their convenience.

Using Performance Assessment as a Culminating Experience

At the close of each year, the school, department, or grade level can publish a book of selected portfolio entries that are exemplars and that demonstrate the highest possible student achievement in writing. Local businesses can place business card ads in the end pages of the book to cover the cost of printing.

Schools can announce an Achievement Day at the end of the semester or school year, during which parents and other community members can come to the school and take part in the student presentations of their portfolios and look at a display of the completed portfolios. In this way, the entire community can celebrate student learning and work together to address the needs still to be met.

At the root of all of these activities to share the results of authentic assessment are the teachers' and students' efforts to make portfolios mean something to someone else. The reason for taking portfolios out of the comfort of the classroom is to ensure that they communicate the learning that is going on in the classroom, department, school, or district. They are a more meaningful demonstration than test scores because they are real artifacts from the actual lessons. Involving the community is a way of enlisting its support and assistance.

Making portfolios public means that what goes on in classrooms—the finished products as well as those in progress—is also public. It is important that when portfolios make their appearances beyond the classroom and school, a teacher or teacher and students accompany them with a commentary and explanation to help the public understand this new form of assessment and what it means. Furthermore, it will be the first time for many that schools have allowed the inconsistencies and anomalies involved in the learning process beyond the classroom door.

By sharing authentic assessment with parents and the community, they will feel that the home-school connection is strengthened, that their input is valued, and that they are viewed as an important part of their student's learning. Authentic assessment helps parents and the community realize that they are an important part of the learning process and that facilitating learning is not just the responsibility of the teacher. The more staff, students, parents, and community members who are involved in the process, and the subsequent revisions that are based on their feedback, the more effective the authentic assessment process will become.

The School Administrator: Leading the Way to Instructionally Sound Assessment

In manufacturing, business, health service, and other fields today, people are seeking to continually improve what is occurring within their organizations or across their fields of endeavor. Many schools across the country also are searching for this flow, this continuity of direction. The use of performance monitoring within and across classrooms presents an extremely powerful tool for teachers to gain both personal and collegial effectiveness. Just at the point when teachers are feeling extraordinary pressures to do more and more with students, authentic assessment models create a greater direction for how to work more competently with individual needs. The teaching and learning process has even more potential to become an art as well as a science.

The school administrator has an opportunity to influence and augment the successful implementation of change at the site level. In fact, having district support for any major change within a district, and having the site-level administrator orchestrating that change within the school, are essential components in making innovations acceptable and powerful enough to become institutionalized. No matter what the project or change, if district- and site-level administrators do not support the efforts, at best they will be just temporary adjustments. There are frequent examples of nationally and state-funded projects that have come and gone. Perhaps we can say that nothing sustains forever except sound principles, and even they must be examined every so often to determine whether or not they still are being articulated clearly in the era in which one now lives.

This last chapter will examine the role of the administrator in bringing forth authentic assessment. What does that person need to know, do, question, and support? We will examine the administrative savvy necessary to move forward in implementing authentic assessment, the collaborative skills necessary to do it well, and the pitfalls that can inhibit or destroy the process.

Gaining Knowledge About
Authentic Forms of Assessment

As a school site administrator, you know that there are always too many needs all vying simultaneously for your attention. To use authentic assessment, consider the following areas that will likely lead you to the next steps in your thinking.

- With interested faculty and community members, work together to determine your school's interests in the area of assessment. It is easy to get caught up in thinking that your school must move completely away from standardized testing and toward authentically assessing students, or that it ought not to move at all in that direction. Find out what your state and district expect of you and your school. By thoughtfully studying issues with your district-level management team, as well as your schoolwide leadership team, site council, or school governance council, you will be much clearer in committing to your school's next directions.
- Seek out training in both the theoretical understanding of authentic assessment strategies as well as the necessary skills needed to use them. You and key members of your staff may wish to attend professional training together. Do not begin

the process of change at the magnitude and political nature of authentic assessment at your school site without some basic tools of understanding.

- Because authentic assessment is a broad term that is being used for several forms of alternative assessment methods, find out exactly what all of the terms mean, as well as their implications to your school, and which are most appropriate for the issues you need to address.
- Strategically assess the human, material, monetary, and time expenditures involved in working toward whatever assessment goals you and your team select. Skipping this process is one of the primary reasons that authentic forms of assessment either do not jell or are not sustained.
- Establish how these human, material, monetary, and time resource expenditures mesh or do not mesh with goals and timelines from your district or state.
- Be realistic in recognizing that teachers need specialized training and long-term, ongoing support in implementing authentic assessment in the classroom.
- Include opportunities for parents and other interested community members to take part in the dialogue about testing and assessment procedures, and for them to work on your school team in understanding how, when, and why specific tools will be used in various courses or grade levels.
- Determine both long- and short-term timelines for your objectives. Comprehension takes time. Do not move too quickly. If teachers and parents cannot understand what is being asked of them or if they disagree with what is being suggested regarding implementing authentic assessment strategies, they will thwart its realization, which could potentially defeat the value that authentic assessment provides your school.
- Authentic assessment is not the panacea for measuring scholastic achievement. When you and your faculty select various forms of authentic assessment, you need to do so for reasons that have been thoughtfully articulated.

The major emphasis in your systemic decision-making efforts is the intent of your use of any assessment. Once you and other key district- and site-level leaders have determined what drives your selection process, you will be ready to begin the process of assisting your full faculty and staff in becoming skilled in implementing authentic assessment strategies.

Collaboration, Professional Development, and Decision Making

There are many materials being published on a wide range of themes related to authentic assessment, and a number of teachers are using portfolios. It is likely that some teachers have become proficient in their knowledge base related to these areas. This may offer a meaningful opportunity for collaborative professional growth among the staff, especially if the culture of the school is receptive to learning about the topic. If they are willing to assist, have your resident experts help in collaborative data gathering to find out the needs, fears, concerns, attitudes, beliefs, and self-defined proficiency of other staff members. It may be that the teachers are interested in learning more deeply about how to implement portfolios, rubric construction or analysis, group projects, or other specific topics. The key is to work together to be sure that both the faculty and you are moving in directions that are meaningful for yourselves, the students and parents, and the community.

Professional staff development on authentic assessment is critical. It needs to focus on how it can support the entire instructional process. At each stage of development, determine how authentic assessment can help to improve instruction and seek out how students can perform tasks that have meaning to them. Administrators, teachers, parents, and students need to understand the selection of appropriate assessment methodology for use in individual classrooms. That is no small task.

There are many types of assessment tools to understand, and each is useful depending upon what result is to be achieved. Some are formal techniques, and some are informal. A few, such as portfolios, exhibitions, demonstrations, performances, and experiments, may be uncommon to the experience of a number of teachers and students.

Once teachers understand what it is that they need for their classroom or groups of students, then they must know either where to obtain that form of assessment or how to construct it. Teachers must learn how to select the most appropriate assessment tools, and then they need to be supported in their use so that they are able to analyze the quality of those tools, especially as they apply to the age, cultural background, learning style, and language proficiency of students. It is true that there are many materials flooding the market. However, as in every area of selecting classroom or schoolwide materials, the more teachers understand about the materials, the wiser they will be in determining what to select. The same authentic assessment tools may be flexible enough to serve many needs if the teachers understand when, how, and why to use them.

Be Aware of Pitfalls

So many blind spots can keep a person from realizing his or her ability to succeed with a new project. These few pitfalls are listed to help you move forward in your efforts. No one wants to make an unfortunate error.

There must be ongoing open and honest faculty communication to achieve continual instructional improvement. An especially important reason to have ongoing interaction of faculty members regarding authentic assessment is to make certain that there is alignment about what is being taught and assessed so that people are not working in isolation. Perhaps more than any time since the one-room schoolhouse, curriculum, skill articulation, and performance assessment across grade or course levels have the opportunity to be viewed as a whole and as a model of continual improvement. When there is a natural current between what students need and their developmental process for optimizing learning success, real opportunities are created for teachers to monitor their flow of instruction.

Teachers need to have the capability to successfully implement authentic assessment practices that are to be used in their classrooms. Time and again, teachers have experienced frustration over being asked to take on projects in which they do not have proficiency, do not buy in, or have not been invited to be partners in the decision-making process—and yet they are expected to implement the projects successfully and professionally. Whether the decision to authentically assess students comes from a state or district mandate, or whether it emanates from the school site, there needs to be sensitivity to the concerns expressed by all faculty members about what they are being asked to accomplish. Teachers must acquire the capacity to succeed, or they may exhibit manifestations of frustration such as confusion, anger, resentment, rebellion, or even defeat. This is not to say that by building capacity, one also demonstrates a corresponding enthusiasm to do what is new—but it is a very important piece of the equation.

There must be a breakdown of the costs and benefits of whatever authentic assessment strategy is initiated. Not only do teachers need time to determine what authentic assessment is and is not as well as what they believe is useful to implement, they also need considerable time to create the appropriate rubrics and analysis structures. This may include using outside consultants and facilitators, instructional aides, and clerical support, as well as considerable time working with one another. Before starting a process that may be too ambitious to succeed because of lack of background, take time together to thoughtfully discern purpose, goals, and direction. Talk with others who have implemented authentic forms of assessment to find out some of the concerns that they needed to work through, think carefully about the resources required, and then proceed.

Build impartiality into the assessment construction. This aspect is one of the single most important variables to success. Teachers who create portfolio guidelines or rubric criteria need to take into consideration student differences in learning styles, language proficiency, and interests. This is no small task and is one of the aspects that, if not done carefully, could backfire in the implementation stage.

Select carefully what you choose to formally assess. Make sure that what you are assessing intrinsically is worth the effort to develop the process for authentically assessing it. If you are not planning to use the assessment over a considerable number of weeks or even months, and if the goals are not serious ones, it likely is not a candidate for the work related to creating an instrument to assess the product.

Be sure that your assessment design fits in with your large goals at the school site. Does it enhance your school improvement program? Will it help you to meet your major long-term school and curricular objectives? If it is not a close match, think seriously about its value to you.

Keep the authentic assessment process separate from your examination structure. If you mix the two, students will not likely see any real difference between the traditional testing format and the new model. By having a clear separation, students are much more likely to be willing risk takers in their work.

The point in describing these possible pitfalls about moving forward to implement authentic assessment is to become wiser and more proactive, cooperative leaders with your faculty in the clarity of your decision making.

Rubrics and Standards

Using rubrics is a way of ensuring that students, teachers, and parents alike know the purpose of the work that students are being asked to do. Creating standards and the steps for achieving those standards leads to higher-level and more complex goals that provide students with information about where they stand currently and what they need to do as next steps. The use of rubrics as a tool for scoring work has the potential for placing the power and responsibility back onto the students to help them know what is being asked of them and how to achieve it.

When teachers use rubrics, encourage them to work together to make the best use of them. Rubrics can come from another source; can be modified and adapted to fit personal course, classroom, or schoolwide needs; and can be created in the district or at the school site. Perhaps the greatest challenge is for teachers and, ultimately, students to translate the performance of various assignments to the rubric fairly and reliably. For this they need support, time, and practice.

Concluding Remarks

When turning to the development of authentic assessment techniques, keep in mind that one of the most valuable goals is in the process of doing the work. It is in the long look at how students grow, modify, and change that teachers and students alike learn more deeply about the student learning process. Also, as they interact with material that is designed to move the students from one level of aptitude to another through an interactive open process, there is likely to be both explicit and subtle changes that take place in student-teacher-parent-administrator interactions because of the dynamics that this work entails.

The entire process of authentic assessment—of seeking the best alternative for determining what and how students are learning, and what sense they are making of their learning—is still in its infancy. However, it has so much potential that if administrators are skillful in supporting teachers and others in their quest for quality, they will achieve far more than if they use standardized testing options as a sole approach to deciding how much learning has occurred.

There is no doubt that we in America live in a very different world from what it was when the parents of students who are in K-12 education today were in school. There is also no doubt that the world for which these students are being prepared is one that has not yet been invented. It takes a great deal of courage to prepare people for walking into the unknown. The life skills embedded in using knowledge, working with knowledge, seeking what is missing, determining what to do in the face of apparent contradictions, knowing when and how to access the many technologies that are emerging, and using the vast number of resources that are available are all important aspects of learning as the students of today become our newest adults entering the 21st century. As administrators begin to open up the avenues of opportunity for teachers to use new models of assessment, and as parents and students learn what is possible through understanding their power, everyone will move toward the next questions. Testing has been an onus to some and a bonus to some others. Authentic assessment has the potential of being a real tool of learning for all, and not merely a static, summative reporting of data or chronicling of progress.

Teachers need to be encouraged to move beyond their beginning work in using authentic assessment techniques, and they will do so most effectively when they feel a supportive encouragement and collaborative working relationship with the administration. The process offers everyone motivation to think and work together in new ways to be successful. By creating a learning environment of continual growth and improvement, students deepen their knowledge base, expand their abilities to think and problem solve, and foster their capacities for active learning, responsibility, decision making, communication, and personal growth.

Annotated Bibliography
and References

These selected titles are a small portion of the materials that are flooding the education market on assessment procedures that offer more complete opportunities for students to verify what they know. We are calling these options for judging the quality of student learning and performance *authentic assessment*. The following list offers opportunities to explore the subject in greater detail. The reader also is encouraged to access technology and to explore current educational journals for a plethora of articles and other resources related to the topic, which might be located under a variety of descriptors, such as authentic assessment, performance-based assessment, alternative forms of assessment, and portfolio assessment.

California Assessment Collaborative. (1993). *Charting the course toward instructionally sound assessment.* San Francisco: Far West Laboratory.

Highlights the work of 22 diverse pilot projects that serve as examples of site-based efforts, along with the costs, impact, and recommendations. This report documents the development of performance assessment strategies in schools and districts throughout California.

Campbell Hill, B., & Ruptic, C. (1994). *Practical aspects of authentic assessment: Putting the pieces together.* Norwood, MA: Christopher-Gordon.

Organizes usable aspects of assessment and evaluation for elementary classrooms, and explores portfolios as well as many techniques for an ongoing basis of collecting and recording information from multiple sources.

Cooper, W. (Quarterly). *Portfolio news.* San Diego, CA: Portfolio Assessment Clearinghouse.

Includes articles and features on a variety of uses of portfolios together with reports of individual projects and issues of concern in portfolio assessment. It incorporates a review of current literature, an information exchange, and other timely topics. This quarterly publication is in its fifth volume.

Costa, A. L., & Kallick, B. (1995). *The role of assessment in the learning organization: Shifting the paradigm.* Alexandria, VA: Association of Supervision and Curriculum Development.

Offers a practical way to focus on assessment not only for student learning but also for the environment in which learning takes place. It shows the role of assessment as a driving force toward continuous learning and improvement in the school system.

Craig, J. R. (1992). *New Directions for Education Reform, 1*(2).

Contains eight articles having different perspectives regarding the nature and role of performance assessment in K-12 education reform. The theme for this issue of the journal is on performance assessment.

Educational Resources Information Center. (1994, Winter). *The ERIC Review, 3.* Rockville, MD: ACCESS ERIC.

Offers an overview of performance-based assessment through articles, descriptions of numerous print resources, and a list of organizations. This issue provides the reader with a wide range of options for finding out more about the subject.

Harp, B. (1993). *Assessment and evaluation in whole language programs.* Norwood, MA: Christopher-Gordon.

Examines effective assessment and evaluation theory as related to whole language in current practice, and includes examples from primary, intermediate, bilingual, multicultural, and special education classrooms.

Herman, J., Aschbacher, P., & Winters, L. (1992). *A practical guide to alternative assessment.* Alexandria, VA: Association of Supervision and Curriculum Development.

Offers clear guidance on the creation and use of alternative measures of student achievement that links assessment with curriculum and instruction and is based on contemporary theories of learning and cognition.

Hewitt, G. (1994). *A portfolio primer: Teaching, collecting, and assessing student writing.* Portsmouth, NH: Heinemann.

Provides samples of student work along with tools for formally and informally assessing portfolios. Suggestions are included for helping students experience personal growth through developing their own portfolio process.

Hymes, D. (1991). *The changing face of testing and assessment: Problems and solutions.* Arlington, VA: American Association of School Administrators.

Reviews problems and proposed solutions to the issue of testing in America's schools. It provides a summary of the evolution of testing in education over the last 100 years along with concerns and alternative approaches currently being posed. Included are sample writing and math rubrics along with suggestions for community involvement.

Jorgensen, J. (1994). *Assessing habits of mind: Performance-based assessment in science and mathematics.* Columbus, OH: ERIC Clearinghouse for Science, Mathematics, and Environmental Education.

Explains the state of performance assessment in mathematics and science education. The book provides descriptions of innovative plans and directions for teachers to use to inform their classroom instruction.

Kutney, B. (1993). *Alternative assessment: Emerging theories and practices at Holt High School.* Holt, MI: Holt High School.

Examines how one high school is implementing alternative assessment strategies in a variety of content areas in an attempt to invent a new school organization. The goal is to more systematically prioritize teaching and learning. The book includes teacher insights and practical examples of alternative assessment practices.

Marzano, R., Pickering, D., & McTighe, J. (1993). *Assessing student outcomes: Performance assessment using the dimensions of learning model.* Alexandria, VA: Association of Supervision and Curriculum Development.

Explains how their model relates to the new lifelong learning standards and content standards. The book includes extensive examples of classroom tasks along with practical suggestions for assessing performance.

Mathematical Sciences Education Board. (1993a). *Measuring up: Prototypes for mathematics assessment.* Washington, DC: National Academy Press.

Illustrates a set of principles that can be used to create mathematics assessment activities for any grade level. This report also describes 13 prototype assessment activities and provides the names of contacts for mathematics education state coalitions.

Mathematical Sciences Education Board. (1993b). *Measuring what counts: A conceptual guide for mathematics assessment.* Washington, DC: National Academy Press.

Examines the recommendations to advance a conceptual framework in mathematics that will help educators who want to develop effective alternative types of assessment. The book looks at equity issues and content appropriateness of various types of assessment, as well as teaching and learning ramifications.

McDonald, J. P., Smith, S., Turner, D., Finney, M., & Barton, E. (1993). *Graduation by exhibition: Assessing genuine achievement.* Alexandria, VA: Association of Supervision and Curriculum Development.

Describes firsthand accounts from members of the Coalition of Essential Schools, who use a strategy called "planning backwards from exhibitions" to create students who actually exhibit and explain the knowledge they have gained through their studies.

Mitchell, R. (1992). *Testing for learning: How new approaches to evaluation can improve American schools.* New York: Free Press.

Provides detailed and vivid descriptions of programs to evaluate student performance in innovative ways. This comprehen-

sive book's clear and persuasive style helps to dispel the fears that abandoning traditional testing measures will increase costs and decrease student accountability.

National Council of Teachers of Mathematics. (1991). *Mathematics assessment: Myths, models, good questions, and practical suggestions.* Reston, VA: Author.

Focuses on examples of assessment techniques that examine students in the thinking and communication that they need to use to solve diverse types of problems through investigation, exploration, and discovery.

Resnick, L. B. (1987). *Education and learning to think.* Washington, DC: National Academy Press.

Provides the reader with background information for understanding the need to teach subject matter so that higher order skills development is a paramount goal of all schooling. This very succinct theoretical book summarizes the linkages between higher order thinking and its relationship to schools.

Wiggins, G. (1993). *Assessing student performance: Exploring the purpose and limits of testing.* San Francisco: Jossey-Bass.

Analyzes traditional test designs and the secrecy and formats that thwart students. It describes how assessment is more than testing, and how intellectual performance is more than right answers if we examine more closely students' habits of mind.